SKETCHBOOK BLACK PAPERS

AT SCHOOL AND HOME

THIS BOOK BELONG TO

....

Made in the USA
Monee, IL
29 May 2022

97194303R10070